When I...

The Dark Side of Mourning:
Grief after the Loss of a Child

By: C. L. SNAPP

When Mommas Cry

The Dark Side of Yearning,
Grief after the Loss of a Child
C. L. Snapp

Copyright 2012 by C.L. Snapp
CreateSpace Publishing

All rights reserved.

Except for use in any review, the reproduction or utilization of this work in whole or in part in any form by any electronic, mechanical or other means, now known or hereafter invented, including xerography, photocopying, recording or in any information storage or retrieval system, is forbidden without the written permissions of the publisher, C. L. Snapp.

ISBN-13: 978-1495936746
ISBN-10: 1495936740

Dedicated to:

My husband, Dicky, you are the true image of Prince Charming. You held my hand, spoke vows of marriage, and never wavered.

My children who like life itself gave me purpose. The challenges siblings face as a family, endures the monumental transformation, after the loss of a child are heroic in nature. I want to take this opportunity to recognize my children, and the strength they have exhibited, and their remarkable ability to keep their brother alive within their hearts.

To my special friends who through their own experience of the loss of a child have contributed precious thoughts, and writings.

To the departed children, I thank you for your lives brought encouragement, hope, resolve, resilience, and empowerment to countless others.

Introduction

My thought is, if you are viewing or have purchased this book, you or a very close family member, or friend has experienced the loss of a child. First and foremost, I want to tell you how very sorry I am that you have been drafted to this club. No one I know would ever volunteer for this journey.

You may not understand my choice of words referring to this as a club. Unfortunately, I don't have a better word to use and this is how you will find my story. This is not your normal 5-stages of grief and find closure book. This is not written for the timid. I will bear my soul and pain *without* apology or asking permission.

The purpose of my writing is, I believe it may help give me strength. Second, I want to share symptoms and stages of grief many are not willing to share because it's a dark, lonely place, and third, if you are annoyed with grammatical errors, and literary techniques you probably won't be comfortable with my writing.

My choice of technique is simple. I write from the heart without the interference of an editor, re-arranging my music.

This is my journey about loss, and I will dance to the music of my grief, my way. It is the single most important message I want you to hear.

This is your journey.

There is no right or wrong way.

There is simply *your way.*

Your child is as unique to you as your fingerprints, and DNA. There is no assembly line, no manufactured coping mechanism. There is no one size fits all.

I am a simple person but not an ignorant one. I have a tendency to let my emotions speak for me. Much of my story will be driven by that emotion, and like any car, you can only have one driver. This journey has revealed places within my soul I did not know existed before losing my son.

My husband and I lost our youngest son, at the age of 22, from a motorcycle accident. He was travelling on a rural, windy road lined with trees, and he miscalculated a curve. He hit a tree and was thrown from the motorcycle. It was a small tree. Medications and machines would stabilize him, and allow him to stay with us for seventeen hours. He never regained consciousness. We held constant vigil in the trauma unit as hundreds of his friends gathered around him.

Acting as a personal security guard, I escorted his friends in and out of the trauma unit throughout the seventeen hours. Our son, Richard considered his friends and family his greatest possessions. It was without a second thought, I made every effort to allow his friends the time both of them needed.

A word of warning before you read this book. It may be too soon. Our son crossed over in June 2006, that was 5 1/2 years ago. It took Elizabeth Edwards, wife of presidential candidate John Edwards ten years to release her book, *Saving Graces,* after the loss of her son. I must be honest, I have not read it, but there are many books out there dealing with the subject of grief. The loss of a child comes as a left hook in life that I call a *Trap Door Transition.*

The loss of a child is not in the family planner, not on the household project list, and turns the family upside down. It is out of the given order of life.

It is the unexpected.

I can only write from personal experience, and perspective. I was born and raised in the United States and for the most part support the traditional Christian belief, but believe we have a lot to learn from the Native American traditions, and Eastern beliefs.

I believe the Universe is much larger than one religion or belief system. In the Scriptures we are told, "My ways are not your ways". I can't relate to the struggles of families living in India and Kenya. The grief suffered by those parents losing children to malnutrition, disease and starvation on a daily basis cannot be compared to my grief.

I would have to think those parents knew they were shadowed by death on a daily basis, and I imagine their hearts were broken when they were unable to withstand deaths grip a day longer. The monumental battle those parents wage against death, as they fight for the very lives of their children is no match for the single phone call my husband and I received on that June day.

I can truly say I tip my hat to those families for the courage and resolve they exhibit.

Throughout this book, I will be sharing my personal, very intimate conversations, thoughts, quotes that feed me, poems that revealed me, personal experiences, and journals in snapshots of what I call *Truth Matters*. The *Truth Matters* will be marked by personal photographs of butterflies, and flowers.

Truth Matters are scattered randomly like salt and pepper, so when you see a photograph, this is your cue to take a break from the flow of the book, and follow me and my special friends on a personal journey through this challenging time of our life.

We just ask for the freedom to express our loss in our words. I don't want to be thought of as a victim. I am not a victim. I also have not lost my faith in God, as so many friends have feared. I am human, and by sharing the most intimate parts of my journey, I hope you can find strength, hope, and courage. I also do not want to offend anyone, and when addressing a subject like grief and the loss of a child there are a million different variables to consider. Some families lose children suddenly through tragedy, others through illness, and many suffer the loss through suicide. My heart goes out to each and every one of you, and it is my hope that anyone sharing in my story understand I am not a professional writer, and I only desire to share my journey, and that we are all one though we arrived here by various means.

This is not a clinical study, not an experiment. This is real life and it's not always pretty. I want to bring the struggle with grief out of the closet, and expose Truths which I believe will provide someone struggling with loss comfort in knowing they are not alone. The struggles that come physically, mentally, and emotionally are, and can be tremendous, and while I admit most everyone experiencing a loss of this magnitude do seek professional counseling, the counseling sessions remain private, and behind closed doors.

I want this is to be a kind of 'in your face' this is what you might experience, and if you do, you aren't alone, it's okay, it's part of the process, the healing, your growth, and you will come through it. You will be battered, torn, exhausted, changed, resolute, transformed, stronger, and passionate.

The Truth is you won't recognize yourself anymore. I am writing this to say, it's okay, I have been there and I'm still there.

As for the aftermath, I was like the many thousands before me experiencing the loss of a child, shortly after the accident I looked for a way to cope. I turned to the internet, and local library for information on grief, healing, loss, suicide, death, and life after death. One of the first books I read was Mitch Albom's, "_Tuesdays with Morrie,_" a non-fiction novel, chronicling his visits with his college professor.

Morrie Schwartz suffers from Lou Gehrig's disease

(ALS). I specifically chose this book to find out if there was anything Morrie might share about preparing to cross over that would provide me comfort in rationalizing the sudden passing. It comes as no surprise that it is also a novel by Mitch Albom, "The Five People You Meet in Heaven", and a made for TV movie adaption released in 2004, that became one of my favorite movies. All I will say about the movie is this, "if you haven't seen this movie, what are you waiting for?"

But it would be a documentary on the History Channel that would provide me my biggest breakthrough. The documentary was the life of Kentucky Prophet, Edgar Cayce. Cayce's life, and work are detailed by Thomas Sugrue in There is a River. My favorite worship song in 2002 was, there is a River.

Coincidence or fate?

It's a song of healing, and hope. When I saw the title of this book three years later, during what is the darkest day of my life, I recognized it as a breadcrumb, food to nourish my soul, and suddenly I found myself knee deep in books detailing Cayce's work.

Edgar Cayce was born in 1877, and is known as the Sleeping Prophet, and the Father of Holistic Medicine. Once I finished _There is a River,_ I followed it up with _No Death, God's Other Door,_ and _Beyond Death, Visions of the Other Side._ I highly recommend these books to anyone struggling with loss, and life after loss. No one; no writer, prophet, minister, therapist, best friend or co-worker, no one has all the answers. You can utilize all of these resources for nuggets of truth and wisdom that will feed you and help you find direction if it's just putting one foot in front of the other just one more day.

The irony is I spent several years before Richard's accident completely engulfed in all things spiritual. My husband had a brush with death in 1998, when a car made a left hand turn in front of him. He was on a motorcycle. While he survived, he spent the next four months completely bedridden, non-weight bearing. This means any time he had to be moved, I used a manual medical hoist to lift him, he had to be turned manually, airlifted from a medical bed to a wheel chair. Non-weight bearing means, the person can carry none of their own weight.

It was a very long, challenging four months. Once those four months were behind us, we faced the challenges of physical therapy and eventually returning to daily routines and his job. This near brush with death sent me into a tail spin searching the Scriptures, television evangelists, and as many churches as I could physically travel to. I couldn't get enough. Every minister had their own interpretation and every church their own method of fulfilling the spiritual hunger. I travelled from San Diego, California to Ft. Lauderdale, Florida eventually expanding to Guatemala and El Salvador.

So I was well aware of what God's word promises me about life, death, and salvation. Richard was still young enough during my spiritual journey that he was many times along for the ride, attending the Brownsville Revival in Florida, where tens of thousands travelled from all over the world to experience what God was doing. The irony is it would be a Kentucky Prophet who crossed over fifty years earlier to sit me down and say, "No death, there is another door".

The first organization, I became familiar with was <u>Compassionate Friends</u>. This organization is geared to support families who have experienced the loss of a child. They have local support meetings, website resources and annual meetings. The loss of our son was an incredible strain on my job, but my employers were understanding, and flexible beyond what would have been required, that I nominated them for an annual Compassionate Employer Award, which was accepted and delivered by a local Chapter Representative.

Whether you surf the internet, build an arsenal of literary works, books and poems, or join support groups or, all of those choices like I did, the one and only thing I want to share is this is your journey.

There is no **right or wrong** way.

There is only *"your way."*

Chasing Jell-O

If you have been around kids, then you know how much most kids love Jell-O. Bill Cosby and cherry Jell-O are synonymous with kids. But have you ever tried to clean up after a two-year old with a bowl of Jell-O, on the high chair tray? It's a daunting task, as you chase it around the tray, it slips through your fingers, and then the Jell-O breaks apart into pieces, turning back into the liquid agent, as the heat from your hands melts it away. This has been my life since that tragic day in June. Just like Jell-O, our family as we knew it had slipped through our fingers. We were once a highly energetic family of six, two boys and two girls, with plenty of sibling rivalry, and daily challenges of working middle class parents and public school.

Now it seems our life, as we knew it had turned into a puddle of Jell-O, and we vessels of clay, under the heat of the storm, were shattered. Tossed around like ships at sea, without a crew.

No direction. No passion. No focus. No future.

At least this is how the dark side of yearning has felt for me. This is a part of the journey many will have to endure. What you have to remember, is this is a journey, not a destination. Our destination remains the gift we receive the day we break free from our human capsule, to soar the Universe, as we reunite with our loved ones.

The lack of direction, purpose, and future are the potholes many parents will experience. Some of my darkest days are because of these potholes.

Writing a book on grief has to be one of the most difficult subject matters to cover. The difficulty comes because each loss is unique, every child is unique, each relationship is unique, and every family is unique. There may be similarities, but it is impossible to duplicate even one, or to write a grief book to encompass every situation.

This is not a one size fits all, there is not even a one size fits most. What I found as I journeyed through grief books, is there was a lot of duplication of grief theories, and I would note things that worked for me and realized, I could not relate to everything in each book nor would everything in each book relate for me. Most of the books I read focused more on grief theory, and not on personal experience. Maybe it was just me maybe I didn't read the right books. Have you had difficulty finding a book you could relate to? The variables brought into a grief situation are as different as day and night.

The most valuable information I have learned in this, is I had to decide this is my journey. There is no right or wrong way to handle your grief, there is only your way. I have also learned, no two people will respond to grief the same way, and the greatest gift you can give yourself or someone you know grieving, is to allow them grief freedom.

Lots of freedom.

I feel like I should repeat that again, *lots and lots* of freedom. Grief needs to be experienced, acknowledged, accepted, expressed, involved, receptive, responsive, outspoken, silent, included, and excluded.

Another important factor when grieving is to throw the clock and the calendar out the window.

There I said it; time will no longer box me in.

It became apparent shortly after the accident, time in and of itself, was not my friend. As the world around us began to return to its routines, I recognized time as my enemy. Time would not allow me to return to what I knew, time would not stand still, as I so passionately did not want things to continue to change, and time would move forward with or without me.

There is no set pace for grief. Grief takes on a life cycle of its own, taking on many phases, stages, makeovers, and personalities. It's enumerable. You can't put grief in a box and time wouldn't let me put it in one either.

Truth Matters

There's no tragedy in life like the death of a child.

Things never get back to the way they were.

Dwight D. Eisenhower
34th President of the United States
(3 year old son lost to scarlet fever)

George Bonanno, a professor at Columbia University has studied grief and trauma for more than twenty years. Bonanno's studies include losses from war, terrorism, abuse, premature death, and the loss of a child. Bonanno wrote <u>The Other Side of Sadness, What the New Science of Bereavement Tells Us about Life after Loss.</u> Bonanno coined the phrase "coping ugly" to describe forms of coping that seem counter intuitive.

I love it.

Coping ugly! The phrase fits me perfectly.

Counter intuitive.

Not mainstream.

The unusual.

The mold breaker.

This is my loss.

This was my son.

This affects my family, my future, my hopes, and my dreams! No scientific study sat at my dinner table on Wednesday nights after a long day at work and school. No scientific study tried to keep up with the laundry for a family of six.

No scientific study made out our annual Christmas shopping list or did our weekly grocery shopping trying to bring home at least one favorite box of cereal or flavor of ice cream.

This is the point, this is my journey.

This is your journey.

It's going to be you standing in the aisle with boxes of cereal on each side, and it may be in the middle of those cereal boxes when you come face to face with that TDT.

Trap door transition.

There is no longer a need for Captain Crunch without the berries in your house.

Your identity lost.

This was who I was, and what I did. I was a mother first. TDT and you will be all alone in that moment, but you won't be alone in your journey.

For me, it was the meat department. As a teenager, and young adult Richard found ways to eat fast and simple, he had friends to meet, cruising to do, music to hear, and well frankly three square meals a day would just get in the way.

So he would come in and fix three sandwiches of the deli sliced turkey and bread (no salad dressing, mustard or cheese). Then finding the largest glass in the cabinet, he would open the refrigerator door, sit the glass on the narrow ledge of the door, and with white milk in one hand and chocolate milk in the other, he would begin pouring both into the glass. Making the white milk, chocolate; and chocolate milk, white, not realizing he was giving his mother a heart attack as I could only imagine the day the glass falls from the narrow ledge of the door throwing milk all over the kitchen.

Funny. Today, I think about this and how monumental a kitchen floor covered in milk seemed at the time. The glass never fell, he had a perfect run. He also provided me a terrific visual of how humanity is not as different as some may think but one within the Universe.

Standing in the lunchmeat section of the meat department became a paralyzing chore. At times the deli turkey would come upon me by surprise, and it would be much like a deer in the headlights.

Frozen.

Run?

Fear!

Guilt.

These emotions and more filled my soul.

Truth Matters

When angry, count to four.
When very angry, swear.

Mark Twain
Samuel Langhorne Clemens
American author & humorist
Twain buried 3 children; a son age 19 months, a daughter age 24; and another daughter age 29
I think he knew what he was talking about.

Do you remember the Etch-A-Sketch? A childhood toy made of plastic with a grey screen using a stylus to displace the aluminum powder on the inside of the screen. You could spend hours dialing those round white knobs, zig here, and zag there.

A picture coming into view, you the architect, engineer, and builder but all it takes for the picture to disappear is to turn the Etch-A-Sketch upside down (and give it a shake or two). My point is 'upside-down'. This is my life after loss. Then you turn the screen back over – nothing. Everything you had built, all your work, your vision gone. My husband and I were on the wrong side of twenty to bring a new baby into the world. This is a very personal and intimate choice. It is your choice. You don't owe anyone an explanation. My personal decision about pregnancy was I could not reproduce Richard.

He was my loss.

Every child unique, one-of-a-kind and this would not erase the loss, it would not bring Richard back. I stared at the blank, grey screen waiting on the energy to turn a knob.

Five years came and went and I am still staring at the grey screen.

Truth Matters

It seems as though the 'kids' are anticipating and awaiting the words to arrive. Many using snippets on their MySpace and Face Book pages - I had told Richard in his 'later' years he would speak the word of the Lord. I just didn't get the itinerary. It's as though I can't get the word out enough - the word that someone who was so real and who made such an impact on me just in the blink of an eye - in a mini-second - in a flash - in a breath - disappears - now I'm left to ponder - 2 days, 2 weeks, 2 months - okay that's enough - no - not one year but now two - okay that's enough - no - now two years and two weeks - now that's enough - two years - unable to comprehend - Then the emotional breakdown again - the fight against reality - the constant struggle that if I

don't give up the fight somehow in some strange way I might just win - and Richard walks back through the bedroom door sticking his head around the corner as he knows I'm awake waiting on him and his dad will be snoring as he peels wallpaper from the wall - then Richard laughs asks what we had for dinner and heads for the kitchen - the picture never changes - or at least I didn't think it would - now I lay here awake waiting and watching for his head - listening to his dad snore but never sound enough to remove the wallpaper, now he wakes often waiting to hear Richard in the kitchen; BUT the laughter never comes.

Cynthia Snapp

In 1969, which I believe to be very recent in the scope of human life, Elisabeth Kubler-Ross wrote <u>Death and Dying.</u> Her theory describes five stages of grief, a largely UNTESTED but popular process, detailing how people deal with death and tragedy.

According to Kubler-Ross, the stages include denial, anger, bargaining, depression, and acceptance. The theory builds a structure by which people can learn to live with what they lost. The theory is clear to point out not everyone will go through all five stages, nor is there a prescribed order.

I believe it is important to note, the Theory came about in the 1960's from observing people who **were** dying and *not* people who had lost a loved one.

I can certainly see where the bargaining stage would exist in this arena; however, once my son was buried, I have to say my bargaining chip had been cashed in.

Quite a controversy exists between Bonanno's research and Kubler-Ross's theory. Bonanno says people who have lost a loved one in fact "do not grieve". These people are in fact **"resilient"**. Bonanno's logic says there is no grief, and therefore no stages of grief through which to pass.

The U.S. English Thesaurus offers this description for **resilient:**

Elastic Flexible   Pliant
Tough   Durable   Strong

Hardy   Resistant   Feisty   Buoyant

Buoyant is our resilience. If you have lost a loved one what word best describes your resilience? Below are synonyms of *buoyant* best describing my life for the last five years?

Floating   Suspended   Hovering

On the edge   On the brink   Volatile

Unpredictable   Erratic   Dismal

Desolate   Despondent

Look if you were hoping for a book resembling a hot fudge sundae, whipped topping, and a cherry, you won't find it here.

I won't apologize for my anger or my disappointment. I am not saying this journey has not offered me and my family opportunities and friendships that otherwise would not have existed. I have a much greater awareness of something as simple as the words I choose to write on a card I am sending someone.

Every word is now chosen with soul searching precision.

Before the accident, I would run in the store, pick out a card, and sign it in the car while sitting at a stoplight on the way to the post office. Dig around in my purse for a stamp, and drop it in the box. Whew!

Truth Matters

Do something worth writing about - or write something worth reading.

*Benjamin Franklin
U.S. Founding Father*

After all it was the thought that counts right? What if it's the last card I send? What if it's the last card they read? What if they cross over before the card arrives? What if I cross over before the card arrives? Cross over? Sure there are times I call it death, but I don't believe my son died, but that he crossed over to a place of Paradise.

A place where tens of millions of living souls of energy, have gone before him. A parallel Universe with multi-levels of existence.

Since death has been engraved on me since birth, it can be difficult to remove this tattoo of belief. I believe in The Light. Whether Jesus is the Light or the Universe is the Light, I don't weigh in on belief systems anymore. Just a few months before Richard's crossing, I found <u>Wisdomkeepers, Meetings with Native American Spiritual Elders,</u> by Harvey Arden & Steve Wall published in 1991.

A photographer and writer team from National Geographic, who spent ten years journeying to twenty Native American nations interviewing tribal Elders. This is an extraordinary spiritual journey into the lives of these Elders. Passage into the afterlife, Mother Earth and creation revealed in a way only these Elders could reveal it.

This book led me to <u>Travels in a Stone Canoe: the Return to the Wisdomkeepers,</u> the first book in the series.

The journey would end with me reading *To Become a Human Being,* by Steve Wall. It is very important to remind you, I found these books **before** my loss but the wisdom within the covers of these books, was the seed planting for the strength, and courage, I would need in the days, weeks, months and years ahead.

I would return to these books, as I searched high and low for answers after the accident. Some of the most powerful words of wisdom were found in the Foreword of *To Become a Human Being.* "When somebody dies, the spirit of that person lives on." "There really is *no* death." Keep in mind, I read these books *before* the accident. Many families find the same comfort reading Scriptures from the Bible. My comfort was found by the truths being shared by others in real time. When you are searching for a tangible truth, it can be difficult to satisfy that hunger with verses I had memorized.

I believe the Scriptures provide healing and are alive, but I needed more, like Thomas, I needed to see the wisdom with my own eyes. I was able to accomplish this with the wisdom shared by Tadodaho Chief Leon Shenandoah, and I will be forever grateful to him.

Truth Matters

As our circle of knowledge expands,
So does the circumference of darkness surrounding it.

*Albert Einstein
1879-1955
German-American physicist*

A couple of months before the accident, I had a dream (nightmare) that showed me Richard would be injured and was leaving. Although, I swallowed hard, I shared the dream with Richard in an attempt to save him. It could have just been a warning dream and the information could actually keep him safe. Richard had a strong spiritual side, and he understood my concern. The dream was a warning, but I would not be able to intervene.

The loss of a child brings so many issues; I never contemplated before the journey. The loss of a child during infancy, in miscarriage or stillborn, neo-natal loss, and sudden infant death syndrome (SIDS); brings with it the loss of dreams. Dreams of rocking chairs, high chairs, teething, crawling, first steps, and first utterance, now lost. The loss of a child in the early years bring the difficult task of having had the experience of bonding and building a relationship, only to have it ripped away by a TDT.

The child is fully able to communicate likes and dislikes. Memories of going to the park, swinging, playing T-ball, and going to Grandma's house for Christmas, now live through photographs and home videos. The loss of a child as they reach adulthood offers an additional struggle, as you battle the years of investment, the accomplishments, the achievements, and the unfinished business. If your loss comes in the form of an adult child, you surely face a fear other parents may not experience.

Security.

Our adult children have grown into mini-me's. As we age, and begin to lean on our children for assistance, in small matters like starting a lawn mower, helping out with a flat tire, or providing transportation, as we undergo medical or physical needs, this loss can also bring a loss of personal security.

This book will be tilted in experiencing the loss of a young adult child. I can only share with you what I have experienced. It is my hope that I don't exclude those struggling with other losses. I hope somewhere in here, there will be a piece of advice, wisdom, or experience that you can find familiar. I hope to share something to give you strength in knowing you may not be alone in your experience.

In most cases, the loss of a child is an unbearable devastation.

Period.

It is my opinion; you won't find the five stage process a complete fit. This is a lifetime process. Your child is part of you. As a mother, you carried this life within you. As a father, you fertilized, protected, and nurtured this life. You are one. One does not merely 'get over' this loss, but as Bonanno says you become resilient. Just as your child was part of your life before the loss, so will your child *and* the loss be part of your life, as you proceed. Now, woven within the fabric of your being, the quilt of your lifetime journey must surely include the loss, to capture the totality of your journey.

Truth Matters

Well my friend another religious and national holiday has come and gone. My husband and I took grandchildren to an Easter egg hunt. The wind was gusting at 25 and the temperature was 50. We were frozen. We took our after the accident adopted dog Sadie and she was the center of attention for the kids. We went through the motions - but my friend - what I have found is there is no "E"-motion. It seems

virtually impossible to get on the escalator of ecstasy that we used to ride. The building momentum - the anticipation - the excitement - 'poof' and its gone. The deafening silence of what has changed. No one has to speak his name. No one has to bring him up in the conversation. No mention of any of it. Yet there it is every day and all day - silence. What part of synchronization still needs to be adjusted? Why am I not in tune? Where is my harmony? When life and death collide. A young 8 year old goes off skipping to play with a friend and a Sunday school teacher driven by evil and a retention pond. Life and death collides. Determined? Destiny? Default? Why do I live to fifty-two and process paperwork by the ton and an eight year old never learns to drive a car? I remain frozen in time. Unlike computers, the more desperate I become to retain and freeze my memories Time continues to eat away - the inability to maintain - humanity does not allow me to retain and restore but forces me to acquire new information forcing out vital information I am trying to retain, memories. Now facing my third year - the inability to keep it as fresh as yesterday - becomes impossible until which time I believe I will be forced to cry uncle - unable to keep that alive in humanity that has passed on to eternal life. For some reason I am far more acceptable of seeing a 95 year old great-great grandmother passing into eternal life - seeing her as complete - a cycle completed - the fruition of her hard work - the end of her shift - her work finished - I was still kneading Richard; he hadn't even begun to rise. He was still searching for his anchor. Why should we deal with arthritis, diabetes and menopause - hell, let's all check out before 30. Leave while we feel good. I wish I could bring myself to tell my mom friend not to cover her head and bury herself but for now this is her way of coping - of surviving - and just because you are not in the public realm today - look I planted gladiolas the first spring - they didn't come back the second year so I thought I had lost them. Then we had an ice storm this winter and now I have glad's popping through 4 inches tall right now - where were they last year - hidden - they had covered their heads - they were withdrawn but they weren't dead. The first thing everyone wanted me to do after the accident was to fight for *the helmet law to be rescinded. But I couldn't. Richard loved riding without a helmet.*

A Multitude of Labels

The Journal of the American Medical Association published a study in February 2007, almost a year after Richard's accident. It was written by experts, at the Yale University School of Medicine, Boston's Dana Farber Cancer Institute; Harvard Medical School Center for Palliative Care, Brigham and Women's Hospital, Department of Psychiatry. After a two year study of over 200 people, who had lost a loved one, the loss was most often the spouse and from natural causes. I want to share what I believe is the most significant finding for people living with loss.

I believe the loss of a child or tragic, sudden loss impacts post-loss behavior on a greater scale, than identified in this study although they mention the difficulties of such loss.

Truth Matters

It is easy when we are in prosperity to give advice to the afflicted.

*Aeschylus
Greek tragedian*

The study performed by Paul K. Maciejewski, PhD; Baohui Zhang, MS; Susan D. Block, MD; and Holly G. Prigerson, PhD, was an empirical examination of the stage theory of grief, which is the accepted model of bereavement taught and applied.

You know the 5 stages of grief to accomplish 'closure'.

What is closure?

The U.S. English Thesaurus describes closure as *closing, shutting down and finality.* Yet the model had never been tested by experience or experiment. The objective was to examine the patterns and magnitude of the five grief indicators, disbelief, yearning, anger, depression, and acceptance.

I'll ask you in common sense terms, even if you find yourself psychologically, physically, and emotionally in a place to accept the loss, do you then shut down and close the door on that portion of your life, your journey?

This is where I have a personal struggle with the five stage theory, and the term closure. I just think they are really seeking understanding. I believe after five years, I have found myself in a place where I can accept the tragedy we experienced, and I am able to do that without bitterness, and with the comfort in believing my son, Richard is still very much alive as his spirit lives on.

I believe he remains with us today, as much a part of the family unit as he was the day he was born.

Truth Matters

Well, I guess that's just the kind of day it's going to be - Let me try this again - I inadvertently deleted my first message which was 90% complete - what's hard to do is to go back and retrieve ANYTHING! I was very serious minded before hitting the 'no' don't save changes button that the heaviness has already begun and now to that you may add frustration - Like I have the time or energy to do anything twice! I hate it just freakin' hate it. I want to believe in the vision, I want to believe that truly all the kids are together and that Richard had the greatest birthday party - why not believe it - I resemble a cheerleader standing on the side-lines anxiously waiting my cue and yet when the buzzer sounds and all is quiet and I am free to go - will I find the strength - when it is all quiet - when I am free to go - the uncertainty and the *unknowing - I know what's here and it sucks - but the uncertainty - no one can say for sure they know any freakin' thing - will I have what it takes - will I have what Richard had - will I?*

Cynthia Snapp

Truth Matters

Everyone can master grief, but he that has it.

William Shakespeare

One area where I struggle with the study is their conclusion that all negative responses are in decline by about six months after a loss. If the responses go beyond six months, the bereaved survivor should seek treatment. I carried a baby for nine months and the study concludes if I have not rebounded and continued on by the end of six months, I should seek professional therapy.

I may have grown up in rural America, and I may not have a PhD but something about that math does not calculate.

I hope the experts will continue their experiment and instead of the majority of the bereaved experiencing loss through natural causes, they will include parents who have lost children on various levels, infants, and adults alike. I also, won't be satisfied with the findings until the effect of trauma and tragedy has major roles within the study.

I read one report that trauma accounts for 6% of the deaths and while that may seem a small percentage, I believe the impact on the family unit makes death by tragedy, trauma more significant than natural causes due to the number of people involved, parents, siblings, grandparents, spouses, children, and friends. The emotional and physical effect of trauma on the survivors and the family unit will have a significant impact on health care and social costs. The loss of the family unit through divorce, the loss of jobs, and earning ability due to depression and illnesses attributed to stress like post-traumatic stress syndrome, chronic fatigue syndrome, suicide, cancer and fibromyalgia.

Truth Matters

Forgive others. Make Peace.

Morrie Schwartz

I am hard pressed to accept a study that concludes I should have recovered from the tragic loss of my son in two months less time, than I carried him in my belly. I guess the experts wouldn't be very happy to find me five years later still *yearning* for my son.

I remember meeting a man at my first Compassionate Friends support group meeting, who had lost a daughter. He introduced himself to me in the elevator and from my demeanour he realized quickly my loss was recent. He shared he had lost his daughter six years earlier, in a car accident. Oh my God, six years, I was filled with panic. I could not survive six years! I told him, "six years, I can't do this six years, not six months, not six weeks".

Now, coming up on our sixth year anniversary, I still think of the father who is coming up on his twelfth. He was still yearning that night in the elevator. I don't doubt that he is still yearning today. I am not alone in my prolonged yearning, and I don't believe it is rare. The study does mention deaths due to trauma or within six months of a diagnosis are more problematic, and the experts suggest a need for evaluation by a mental health professional and potential treatment.

Truth Matters

Grief makes one hour, ten.

William Shakespeare, English Poet
Truth Matters

Every day is a struggle. Everyday another mountain to climb. Will I tire? I have another mom friend who lost a son. She's lucky. She got the cancer. She will see her son much, much sooner than I will. The irony is she found beauty in everything from small babies, children and flowers after the loss of her son. The first few months after our tragedy the MOST difficult thing for me was to be in the middle of the grocery store and see the 3-5 year olds riding in the car buggies. Why? Richard was 22. He would not be happy that I am seeing him as a 5 year old. My mom friend passed away December 2008 her suffering is finished. She barely had the cancer a year. She took treatments and wanted to live. She lost all her hair. She wanted to live. She passed.

Does this make any sense? I want to move on and yet I am bound to the desires of a Higher Power. I have another mom friend suffering from the loss of a son who talks of suicide all the time and she may well act upon those thoughts one day. The pain is unbearable for her. She has many days she is unable to get out of bed. Do I report her to the local authorities so they can drug her up; confine her for a week and then return her to her bed? I have been on the medications to ease the pain now for over two years yet the pain does not go away it only makes life tolerable! No one should ever stand on the other side of the street and judge the decisions of someone else. Until you cross the road and walk in their shoes - every moment of every day of every week of every month of every year of every decade of their entire life - don't begin to pass judgment on their decisions. My decision will be to continue to climb the mountains to live up to what Richard would want of me - not to be a tragedy, not to fall to the grips of tragedy. One time we had a mouse get into the house to have her babies and Richard captured each baby mouse and carried them outside. Life.

Meltdowns come out of nowhere, like yesterday. The sun was everywhere, the motorcycles were humming, friends were riding, people were scattering, the energy of spring and the hope and life it brings with it was tangible, yet everywhere I looked it became a reminder. A reminder of what was missing. Unlike my mom friend I haven't reached the point to find the beauty beyond the pain. How do you get to the place where you don't see the missing piece of the puzzle but you see the whole picture? The one filled with memories and family members gone long before Richard. I have even used my 'mother voice' to try to get Richard to show me a sign - talk to me - come in a dream. After all he knows how to do that. I think I am too desperate to hear.

Cynthia Snapp

I did attend therapy sessions, and today I am under the care of a Psychiatrist MD, but I am no longer on anti-depressants. Immediately following the loss, the treatment is usually the administration of anti-depressants. The administration of medications will not diminish the parental yearning, but for some they are a tool that enables them to continue in everyday routines. The medications helped keep me grounded, in a way they switched auto-pilot back on while my mental, emotional, and physical body came to terms with reality. The experts admit individuals may cognitively accept the death of a loved one, but they may still pine (i.e. yearn) for their loved one and experience the pain of loss.

Truth Matters

Yearn - ing

-noun   1. Deep longing accompanied by sadness, deep pity, sympathy, melancholy desire, unfilled need

(Do not confuse this with self-pity, this is NOT self-pity)!

On Richard Allen's birthday after the accident, I published this in our local paper.

A Tribute to Life

(Life; "vibrant, full of energy, sparkle, resilience, spirit)

To most of us his life seemed to short. He was a son, a brother, a nephew, a cousin, an uncle and most of all a friend. We knew him as the kid on crutches who struggled for years with rheumatoid arthritis and a lover of music never leaving the house without a CD in his hand. He was the defender of the defenceless; a Good Samaritan changing flat tires for stranded strangers and offered rides to those in need. To some, he was the quick oil and lube guy at Valvoline, the voice in the dairy case at Kroger, and a delivery many for Cables. To others, he was the redneck on a 4-wheeler, a jet ski, behind the wheel of a pickup truck or the Mickey D's mustang, with ripped jeans and untied boots, popping wheelies in Terry's parking lot and cruising The City or The Rocks. He was the survivor of a .44 bullet, installed heating & cooling systems, an electrician's helper, a painter, manhandling a fork-lift at Quebecor, a confidant, a comedian, worked with Park's Landscaping and had a soft heart for a pretty girl. An avid swimmer, boater, took his

Marlboro's and Bud "Light". He liked his steak rare, drank milk by the gallon, was a fan of Homer Simpson and swam against the tide of tradition. Always found the good in people choosing not to sit in judgment of others and persuaded many to show mercy and offer second and third chances to those who had wronged them. He completed eighth grade in twelve weeks and never missed a session of summer school in high school. He was voted the "worst case of senioritis" graduating with his Class of 2002. To most, he was the one full of life and light, heading to the Clay City drag strip with friends instead of cleaning his room, a work of art in a ballerina costume or wearing a local beauty queen's crown, and he was a father's best friend. You wouldn't find him without a cell phone, he told his momma everything (just AFTER the fact), and he always remembered to say thank you. This and more would be life as normal - full of adventure, excitement, laughter, challenge, disappointment, surprise, hope, family, friends and he was convinced one day he would find the Garden of Eden. Today, he would challenge us to experience what life has to offer as he truly loved life. He was a living example that friends and family are life's treasures. There is a poem that says when we die it is not what we take with us but what we leave behind that is important; but I have witnessed that you do take something with you when you die; you take the hearts of those you touched while you were alive. So it is that we remember him, our friend this March 31st on what would have been his 23rd birthday. We know heaven has not been the same since he arrived and one day we will all be united; just believe.

FLY ON!

Cynthia Snapp

Auto-Pilot Engaged

In the immediate hours following a loss, it seems life is on auto-pilot and you are a mere passenger. If the loss is sudden, major decisions have to be made with little or no forethought. Those decisions began for us within minutes of Richard's passing, minutes within leaving the hospital. They actually came on our cell phone as we were trying to drive home. The call was from the hospital.

Shaking so hard it was difficult to answer the phone, I thought oh my God, what has happened, did we leave the hospital too soon? After all, I was almost sitting on Richard when he passed; we stayed quite some time, stayed with his friends who had remained on vigil. The Coroner had been called. Should we have waited for him to arrive and followed behind him? We chose not to, because it would have been so painful for us to know Richard was in there and there was nothing we could do to help him.

I turned to my husband, "it's the hospital." We looked at each other in shock. My husband asked, "Do I turn around?" I turned back to the phone. It was a very young man asking about organ donations. Organ donations! Oh my God, I told my husband they want to know if we want to donate Richard's organs! Our heads were spinning. Why had this not been addressed at the hospital? They call you on a cell phone, while you are driving a car, trying to grasp the fact your son just died, you're driving away from the hospital bed where he is laying.

Are you kidding me? No, it's true. We had been on a life support vigil for seventeen hours, and no one mentioned organ donation, and we certainly weren't thinking organ donation.

Under normal circumstances when you aren't in the middle of a life altering situation, I think most people support the idea of organ donation. Richard's aunt was the recipient of a donated liver. She had received a liver transplant several years earlier, and this gift added ten more years to her life.

In the heat of the biggest battle of your life, you are not expecting to get a call on your cell phone, minutes after leaving the hospital asking for pieces of your most prized possession.

Truth Matters

I can't stop, rewind or speed up the clock. The very ticking sound annoys me. Time has taken control of my life. Twenty months after the accident Richard's toothbrush and razors are still on the bathroom vanity. There are days I feel like people and noise suffocate me. It's okay. There are days I don't take a shower or wear makeup. It's okay. There are days that I do. The cemetery is a lonely place. I recognize every parent who comes to the cemetery who has lost a child. The first winter after Richard's passing my mother nurturing kicked in and brought with it a complete and total meltdown. Richard would be so cold - it would be so dark and he would be alone. Very, very difficult reality to

face. I know he's not 'there'. Try telling that to a mother who worried about a coat and gloves for twenty-one winters. Time moves. Not backward and not early - it just moves.

Cynthia Snapp

After what seemed to be a lifetime, I answered yes. Yes, we will donate organs. What I was not expecting, was the laundry list that would begin firing at me like an AK47. I was under the impression the request was for major organs, heart and liver, after all I don't have a medical background. When asking for organ donation, they list every fiber, tissue, nerve, and organ. If it's a body part they're asking for it. If I sound somewhat frustrated at the process I was.

I didn't even know what some of the things were this caller was asking for. Did he really have to list the entire human anatomy? After several minutes of anatomy inquiry, he listed off several diseases, and asked if Richard had any of these diseases to our knowledge. One of the diseases was rheumatoid arthritis. My response was yes, he did. You could feel the disbelief through the phone, because the caller knew the deceased was twenty-two years of age. Confused the young man asked again, "he had rheumatoid arthritis?" Yes, he did. He had Juvenile Rheumatoid Arthritis. You could feel a chill in the air. The caller asked to put me on hold while he confirmed some information. Returning to the phone, the caller said, "Ma'am I am so sorry, but we are unable to accept the organ donations, if the donor has had rheumatoid arthritis because it is a systemic disease, and touches every part of the body." You are freaking kidding me, right?

You just called me minutes after losing my son, on a cell phone, while we are trying to drive home, to ask me if you can dissect my son, I painfully withstand minutes of an anatomy class with terms I am completely unfamiliar with, while you confirm donation of every part of the human body, and you wait until you have taken me completely through this horrific ride to verify potential negative disease impact?

Don't you think maybe, just maybe you should verify any negative disease impact to organ donation BEFORE I had to agonize over your taking my sons body apart? In complete and total disbelief, I hung up the phone. I looked at my husband who was still wondering if we needed to turn around and go back to the hospital and I said, "Richard can't donate his organs, after all that, the arthritis rejects him as a donor."

The disease had gotten him again. It stole the early days of his childhood as he was unable to participate in basketball and baseball with his friends, due to the pain in his hips and knees. To compensate for this on Saturday mornings, I would drive him thirty miles to participate on a youth bowling league. I'm sure not all organ donor families had an experience like ours, but I wanted to share this with you as part of the dark side, sometimes even the most thought out program hits a snag.

I guess it was just not our day.

Truth Matters

I finished a book called "diary" that I just randomly chose at the library when I couldn't find a book I'd wanted. A young man failed in his attempted suicide and left a wife and daughter and the wife kept a "coma diary" and throughout the book she would write things like "just for the record, today's weather is partly furious with occasional fits of rage." Today the weather was mostly lonesome with a 100% chance of tears.

A Ping in the Ethernet for a Special Mom Friend

Thank God for auto-pilot. There is a lot to be said about how our bodies respond to shock. Decisions have to be made on a large scale. These aren't temporary decisions but the decisions you make during this time, will live with you forever. I just want to say, don't beat yourself up if six months after the loss, you realize you left someone out or you forgot to include one of your child's favorite items in the memorial. Guilt will try to creep in like a burglar in the middle of the night.

My husband and I chose to have a traditional funeral service for Richard. We met with a local funeral home director choosing a traditional burial and selected his casket, a Midnight Blue, music ministers and a cemetery plot.

Richard had older siblings who already left home and established their own families. Richard was living at home, was not married and had no children. My husband and I decided to purchase our burial plots when we bought Richards. His dad said he did not want Richard to be alone. There were two things I realized only after auto-pilot shut off, I had failed to do.

I failed to acknowledge my step-brother in the obituary. While I justify the oversight by the fact he was an adult when our parents married, so we didn't grow up together, and he wasn't a strong presence in Richard's life. I still felt really bad because you can't go back and edit an obituary six months later.

Second, I forgot Richard's socks.

The last thing a mother ever thinks about when she's butthole deep in laundry on Saturday mornings is laying out the last clothes your child will ever wear, ever. Not once in all my Saturday mornings, and hundreds of hours in the laundry room, did I ever think about the day I might have to pick out that last outfit.

I forgot to take socks to the funeral home. I didn't realize it until auto-pilot shut off and it was weeks later. You can't call the cemetery workers when you remember, and well you know the rest. It ate me alive about those darned socks. Richard always wore socks. How could I have forgotten his socks? I did. It's just that simple. I forgot his socks.

You may have already thought of someone you unintentionally left out. I never addressed it with my step-brother. I hope he understands the difficult circumstances and realizes it was an innocent oversight. There may be something you wish you could have done differently with your service, I think we all do. We did the best we could, with the time we had, under the most difficult circumstances of our life. It's okay. I believe all our kids are simply saying, "Chill out its okay, you did great!"

Can you think of something during times of reflection you wish you had done or not done as you prepared your goodbyes? There are probably thousands of us right there with you. Don't you just have to know those kids are scratching their heads in wonderment why we are so stressed about it?

Truth Matters

I was seldom able to see an opportunity until it had ceased to be one.

Mark Twain

Once you have finalized the memorial, and everyone goes home, the decisions don't stop there. Every loss, and the circumstances surrounding the loss, will impact your responses to those decisions. For me, it would be weeks before I returned to work. During those weeks, I drowned myself in photographs of Richard. If I made one trip, I made a thousand to the local photo shop making copies of pictures with Richard in them. I was paralyzed with fear that if I didn't have a picture, I didn't have anything to hold on to. If I had lost every single photo I had of Richard, I believe I would have died from hyperventilation. I could feel myself shutting down and my breathing would get very shallow at the very thought I had lost or misplaced a picture.

Every room in our house began to fill up with pictures, until it was so out of control, my husband said I had to stop, there were just too many. He said there wasn't a single spot in the house where he didn't turn and see Richard, and it was too difficult for him. So, to try and prove him wrong that there weren't too many pictures, I counted them. There were almost one hundred pictures of Richard scattered around the house.

He was right. Had he not said something I would have just kept going, I was out of control. I couldn't have enough pictures of him; I had to be able to see him wherever I looked. Having Richard's picture in front of me at all times was my way of feeling safe. In an effort to reduce the number of pictures around the house, to give my husband some relief, I picked two pictures and put them away. I know, two but at the time that was monumental for me.

What are you holding on to? Many parents will sleep with their children's clothes or a blanket. Is there a personal item of your child's you carry with you at all times? I had a charm with Richard's photograph imprinted on it and wear it on a necklace. I have worn it every day for the last five and a half years.

I became very fanatical. You may find this very hard to believe. You may think it impossible, but I became a fanatic about Richard's gravesite. With the exception of a few days, my husband and I, and the kids went away shortly after the funeral; I visited Richard's gravesite everyday day for three years. Sometimes I would stay for an hour other times I would stay ten minutes.

Fresh flowers were on Richard's gravesite every day for the first year. I would go every day to remove any flower that looked like it was dying. The sight of anything dying was disgusting and I felt like it was an insult to his memory. I would sit and pull single blades of grass, keeping the area perfectly manicured. One day, just days after the funeral, I went to the cemetery and still sitting in my car, I was engaged in a mental battle of epic proportion. The dirt mound was still prominently poised above the grass. I needed to get Richard out of there. I don't know if I needed to look at him again or hold him to shake myself out of this nightmare or to rescue him.

I was going to dig him out of there with my bare hands. Yet, as I sat in the car, the other side of my brain was telling me if you get out there and start digging that grave up with your bare hands; someone is going to call the cops.

What are you going to accomplish? Before you can get him out of there, they will have the cops out here, and they will haul you off to the psych ward and you still won't get Richard out of there.

I warned you early on, I was going to tell you the truth.

Am I crazier than other parents who have suffered this loss? I don't think so. I think this is actually quite normal. What I think is, that no one wants to talk about it. No one is willing to get it out of the closet. It's hard for me to share this with you. It's hard for me to go back there now five years later, and now as I am sharing this with you, tears are pouring down my face.

I could still go out there and with my bare hands dig him up but the outcome wouldn't be any different today, in fact it would be worse, because I could have dug faster five years ago! Okay that's it for now the tears won't stop and I need to go blow my nose.

I just want you to know that if you have had thoughts like this, if you have been there in that same tug of war it's okay,

I was right there with you. Whether it was a week ago, a month, a year or ten years, I know the pain and I know the struggle, and yes it still hurts.

What the grief theories and studies don't tell us, is what to do with the parental instinct to protect and nurture. From the time of our awareness of conception, until today (not the moment of loss) even today, the instinct to protect and nurture is with us.

Have you found a grief book that tells you what to do with that? I hope you did. I haven't. So I still struggle with that today. What I have found is now my protection radar is for his memory. Do you remember MC Hammer's song, "U Can't Touch This"? I wondered if there was a mother in the animal kingdom who would fiercely surpass my level of protection over my son's memory. The Smithsonian Magazine did an absolutely beautiful article in May 2011 "What Animal is the Best Mother?" I am going to provide the link for you.

http://www.smithsonianmag.com/science-nature/Ask-an-Expert-What-Animal-is-the-Best-Mother.html

Most of us have been encouraged by the wisdom of others, who may or may not have experienced a loss. Many times, the encouragement comes in the form of what we should do to recover, move on, get over it, and find closure. This article hits the nail on the head right off the bat, when it directs attention to the heated debate over parenting styles. Those styles don't change based on circumstances. Your style of parenting should be the one steady factor as you proceed on your journey. Why should you change who you are now?

This journey is about you. Remember there is no right or wrong way it should only be your way. When you find the inner strength and stand up to the many voices, remaining true to yourself is when you will find the personal strength to continue.

In my good ole' southern terms, if I had someone placing excessive pressure on me to perform to their standards I would simply reply, "You don't have any dogs in this fight." Depending on where you are in your journey, you understand my choice of word, fight.

Kudos to elephant mothers, who endure a 22-month pregnancy and polar bears who must double their body weight for a successful birth according to the article. The article quotes Craig Saffoe, a biologist and curator from the Smithsonian's National Zoo that if you are looking for the **best moms,** you have to consider those who protect their young and ensure survival. Saffoe also notes in the animal kingdom the infants are so fragile and not every animal is great in the handling of their young.

Saffoe talks about the *maternal instinct* and while it kicks in, it is still up to the animal to listen to it. Saffoe compares the animal kingdom mothers to people commenting, "There are great mothers and there are not so good mothers." It's a choice.

A mother's choice.

This brings us back to your journey and your choice. If my losing Richard gives me but one gift, it is that I want you to know how very important it was to him that people not bend under the weight of others opinions.

Richard was passionate about being yourself. He experienced his share of bullying. As a boy spending much of his grade school years walking with the assistance of crutches, he depended on friends willing to help him carry a lunch tray or a heavy book bag. To the bullies, he was a target of weakness and vulnerability. When the disease went into remission in middle school, and Richard had a growth spurt taking him over 6 feet tall in high school, there were moments of reckoning for those bullies. The experience gave Richard the life skills and desire to protect the vulnerable and the weak.

Truth Matters

No one ever told me that grief felt so like fear.

C. S. Lewis
Irish author

The maternal instinct Saffoe talks about does not turn off like a water faucet. To prove my point, Saffoe shares an incredible story of a female cheetah named Zazi, who in April 2005 gave birth to six cubs, one of which was stillborn. Saffoe and his team watched Zazi care for the stillborn cub as though the cub were alive. Zazi groomed both the living and the stillborn cub and when she moved the sibling cubs she moved the stillborn cub with them. Saffoe said it was, "being a good mother beyond what was reasonable". In the wild, Saffoe said the protection of the stillborn cub could have proved to be dangerous for Zazi and the sibling cubs, as she expended energy moving the stillborn cub she may have needed for herself and the siblings. Saffoe admits most carnivore moms in that situation would have consumed the offspring.

Saffoe believes Zazi is most likely, the best mother he has ever seen. He admits this is unusual and colleagues share terrible stories of cheetahs in other situations which bring us back to the undeniable fact, it's an individual choice.

But, when addressing the original question of who in the animal kingdom is the best mom, Saffoe admits it would be the gorilla. Saffoe says he can't think of a single case of a gorilla being a neglectful or bad mom.

So, if you are still moving the child you lost along the journey with you, I want to let you know you are not alone. Zazi and I, are right there with you. Living examples of a mother's choice and a mother's instinct. I am beyond grateful to the Smithsonian National Zoo for this story. I believe it supports my personal belief there is no right way or wrong way and my desire to continue to nurture and protect long after the loss while it may be unusual, it is not something I need to seek treatment for or explain to those who may not understand.

The Good, Bad and Ugly

I have tried to figure out a way to be as transparent about my journey, after the loss of a child, as I could without including this chapter.

It's my fear, someone reading this book will take away that what I have experienced is either the way everyone will experience loss, or my experience is rare. The Truth Matters fact is, I believe it is neither. I don't believe everyone will experience what I have, I also believe there are mothers who have experienced a much broader range of responses, and I don't believe any of this is rare or requires long term treatment programs.

What I hope to see is, more mothers sharing their personal journeys. I am also open to opportunities to assist mothers with that task. Certainly the internet, Microsoft and eBook publishing have made it possible for mothers, who may have never considered this before. Yet, there are thousands of mothers who may not have the computer skills to complete such a project.

Every mother has a story. Every story is valuable.

I am not a psychologist or a professional therapist, and I am not offering any professional or medical advice, but I am an experienced grief stricken mother. What I have experienced on a personal level after the loss has enabled me to acknowledge how a TDT can humble you.

I shared spending several years studying spiritual issues and trying to get my personal spiritual house in order. I never thought I was perfect but I did my best to help my community, strangers in need, family members, and live by the golden rule, "Do unto others as you would have them do unto you."

Truth Matters

I have "become a hermit with the rare exception of going to the garden and the random "safe" gatherings of my son's friends and I am not amazed that it doesn't get any easier but I am confounded that it actually gets harder. People don't want to hear that they just want us better and happy and mostly, they just want us to pretend.

A Ping in the Ethernet to a Special Mom Friend

The purification process of my TDT, allowed a very ugly piece of me to be revealed. The grocery store offers good and bad avenues for mothers suffering from the loss of a child. In the early weeks after Richard's passing, I was in the grocery store and when I turned an aisle I came face to face with a mother and a very young child, age 3-5 riding in the big plastic buggy car, and I was overwhelmed with an emotion of jealousy. What I couldn't understand was Richard was a young adult far beyond being a toddler. Finding myself face to face with the toddler engaged thoughts of why? Not why me?

Just why, lots of why's. Why bother with all the hard work, school and vacations? Why bother with life in general, if after all the due diligence of protecting him, when he could not protect himself, that when he becomes independent, the Universe turns against me? After years of nurturing, where is my harvest?

What lies ahead for these toddlers? Will their lives be cut short? Are they going to die tragically? Thoughts of actually taking one of the young kids raced through my mind. I'm fifty years old, I never once ever thought of taking someone's child.

Dark.

Dark, ugly thoughts I never knew existed within my soul were surfacing. The good thing is these thoughts were very temporary. I must admit there were times I was terrified to go to the store that I would cross paths with a child and thoughts of envy, jealousy, and even kidnapping would rear their ugly faces, and I would freeze in fear.

I don't remember exactly how long I experienced this, but if this has happened to you, I just want to comfort you by letting you know, I've been there and done that. Battles in the mind of epic proportion appear out of nowhere. The only thing I could figure out about the age issue was I think of

Richard as our little boy since he is the youngest of four. If you are experiencing something similar to this now, breathe. Simply, breathe. The good news is it is temporary. I don't believe it lasted more than a couple of weeks, so if what you are experiencing has lasted longer than that I would ask you to share this with your doctor. I know. I was scared. I was scared they would commit me to a hospital. Five years later, I am still scared to share the story for fear of the backlash I might get from parents or professionals.

The struggle was, how can I be transparent and share the dark side of yearning, if I wasn't willing to share the full story.

I opted for Truth Matters.

Truth matters

He who learns must suffer, and even in our sleep pain that cannot forget falls drop by drop upon our heart.

And in our own despair, **against our will**, comes wisdom to us by the awful grace of God.

Aeschylus
Born 520 BC
A Greek tragedian whose work has survived, he is often called the Father of Tragedy.

Another dark area of my life after the loss surrounds the fear of divorce. There are as many statistics on this as you are willing to read. Some experts and bloggers sensationalize the 75% and higher, divorce rate among married couples who experience the loss of a child. The national organization Compassionate Friends, who provides support for families after a child dies, released a report in 1999 stating 72% of parents who were married at the time of their child's death are still married to the same person. So, I am not even going to attempt to discuss statistics here. After 5 1/2 years since our son's accident, his dad and I are still married.

Just as life forever changed, our family forever changed. Our marriage forever changed, our lifestyle forever changed. Our priorities forever changed, our opinions forever changed. Our perception forever changed, our desires forever changed. Our greatest desire is for our children to live long, laugh much and love often.

Second to that, our greatest desire is to go home, wherever, whatever you call home; Paradise, Heaven, Universe or Galaxy, whatever your belief is about what happens to a human being when our bodies die.

This is our second greatest desire. Neither one of us feel connected to this world anymore. Is that normal? It's our normal. I get a lot of criticism for feeling this way, because I do have living children and grandchildren. This is the quandary, my sense of feeling connected has absolutely NOTHING to do with my kids or my relationship with my kids, nothing!

My disconnection is with the world, the world system, the continuity of the law of life and death. It goes to my priorities have changed. I participate in and witness so many things, I consider mundane in the scope of life. It is this, from which we feel disconnected. We don't get over the top excited for the newest release, the most recent upgrade, or the latest version of anything. It is simply a disconnection from the materialism of this world. Is that normal, not really. It's our normal.

If you thought marriage was hard work before the loss, hang on because you are in for the ride of a lifetime! I am only sharing what we have experienced and my prayer is you haven't had to experience ANY of this!

Seriously, I really hope you haven't and you won't. My reason for sharing this is for someone who might be struggling, feeling isolated and wondering if there is something wrong with them. I really don't feel like there is something wrong with me. I feel like I have been deeply wounded, lost my sense of security, my identity challenged and struggling to understand my purpose and my future.

The routine struggles of a successful marriage are magnified a thousand times after the loss of a child. I have found two of the most important areas I believe have helped my husband and me so far in our journey, and that is **flexibility and patience.** Sure you need those in any marriage but you will need to dig down a lot deeper now.

The one thing most grief experts agree on is the uniqueness of response to grief. Everyone will respond differently. The degree of flexibility and patience you are willing to submit to, will determine the level of your success, and ability to work with each other as you travel through this difficult time, instead of adding another difficult layer of obstacles. I'm sure there are times my husband leaves the room, takes a nap or turns the television up, to let me be me. I have personally honed my skill of biting my tongue, reading a book and taking the dog outside; to give him much needed space.

Truth Matters

Grief drives men into habits of serious reflection, sharpens the understanding, and softens the heart.

John Adams
2nd U.S. President

It's not easy. I think it's against human nature; to stretch out of the way of someone else, to bend instead of break, sometimes drawing a line in the sand gives us greater control. The one thing, we feel we lost in addition to our child.

I now feel controlled. One very intimate area of lack of control is during our intimate times together. It takes an incredible amount of energy to hold it together, as you go about your daily life. It takes an incredible amount of strength to maintain composure. When a woman experiences an orgasm she relinquishes all control. She no longer controls the strength and the muscles to maintain composure.

If you are under constant constraint to hold in gut wrenching pain, that rarely leaves your soul, when you attempt an orgasm, the gut wrenching pain you have been holding in explodes. The grief you are trying to keep composed, is now free to express itself.

This is where my husband has exhibited flexibility and patience on a level, I believe is rare. When this grief explodes, it's childbirth like whaling, the sheer agony and pounding of fists would be enough to send any partner packing.

Ugly, very ugly. It isn't easy sharing this with you, but I feel like I need to. I opted for Truth Matters.

Truth Matters

For some moments in life there are no words.

David Seltzer
Willy Wonka and the Chocolate Factory

I feel like there must be other women, who when they reach orgasm during intimacy, are forced to let go of the muscle control they have put in place to maintain composure, to hold in the pain. I just have to believe this is not unique to me. The severity was of course much worse just after the loss; the good news is we have begun to see a slight improvement in the severity of the explosions. The good news is my husband has not been willing to give up on me and to walk away. He has been patient and resolved. He has been understanding and recognizes the depth of the pain, and he probably hopes for the day, I will eventually be able to get it all out. So far, five and a half years and counting. For now, it seems he is willing to stick around for that day.

Priceless.

Have you struggled with intimacy? Where do you think the struggle stems from?

Fear?

Anger?

Disappointment?

Our intimate relationship has changed, but I won't say it has changed forever. Although, it is an added challenge, I want to believe we are stronger as a couple, willing to meet every obstacle of this journey together and to the end.

You have probably realized by now a dark topic I haven't talked about. Suicide. It will be extremely difficult for me to talk about suicide, even though it is a frequent thought to most, if not all parents, who have suffered the loss of a child. The reason is, mothers of children whose lives were lost to suicide. How transparent can I be, and not cause more harm to a mother suffering from this loss.

It is my desire to respect and honor these mothers, just as I honor the mothers in India and Kenya for their courage which is why I am choosing not to fully disclose my experience with thoughts of suicide. Except to say, my husband and I both have the thoughts. My personal reason for such thoughts is simply to end the pain. Nothing else. Anything, to end the pain. It has nothing to do with quitting or not loving our other children as much as we love Richard, only to end the pain.

According to research, parents are at a heightened risk for suicide especially in the month following the death of a child. Our closest family members and friends would agree with the research. I am going to opt for Truth Matters. During the first month after Richard's passing, I was still on auto-pilot. I was still in shock. I have to say our house was on suicide watch. Our children, our siblings called or came by the house almost hourly for the first month. In fact, our oldest son remarked while we were still at the hospital, just moments after Richard's passing, "Don't you even think about doing anything." Oh yeah, there was suicide watch. I opt for Truth Matters. I was not thinking suicide.

Not then.

Truth is, I wasn't thinking anything. I was numb. It would be weeks later before the thoughts and desires to end the pain came. They have been like waves of the ocean ever since. Always crashing against the shore, beating me, and crashing against me like the ocean crashes against the shore. One more crashing wave, maybe this time she'll crack. The good news neither of us have, not yet.

I wish I had words of great wisdom for mothers who have lost children to suicide, but I haven't experienced your pain. It's why I think every mother has a story and now with the world of Kindle and eBooks, I believe you can be a source of strength, hope, and courage for mothers who have experienced your pain. I can be angry at the crotch rocket (speed bike) motorcycle industry or the Kentucky State Law that allowed my son the freedom to ride without a helmet. I realize it was his choice not to wear a helmet, but the law gave him a choice. I don't get too angry over the law, when I have to also recognize the damage to Richard's body. He would not have survived the catastrophic internal injuries. We can all find numerous details of what took our children, to be angry with. The good news is, I came to terms with the fact the anger would not bring Richard back.

Do you ever feel like people around you misread your emotions? I think a lot of people believe I am angry. I opt for Truth Matters.

I'm not angry.

I am yearning.

Yearning for what once was. Yearning for a son to ask me what's for dinner, or calling to say when he will be home, yearning for our family to be whole, and healthy, yearning for the career, a wife and children for a son, who I nurtured from birth.

Angry?

Not anymore.

Truth Matters

"Somebody should tell us, right at the start of our lives that we are dying. Then we might live life to the limit, every minute of every day. Do it! I say. Whatever you want to do, do it now! There are only so many tomorrows."

Pope Paul VI
Italian Pope
1897-1978

Oh, Dad, It's Just the Plane

The first dream Richard's dad had after his passing, these were the words Richard spoke, "Oh Dad, It's just the plane." Richard had never been on a plane.

There were a few opportunities for Richard to join us on flights when he was a teenager, but he wanted to stay home and have friends stay with him.

Dad it's just the plane.

This was the first 'sign' we received, Richard was alive and well. His choice of words, "Oh, Dad" was his way of telling him to stop worrying.

My thoughts when I contemplated this book were, "surely the world doesn't need one more book on grief and the healing process." So why for months has my husband or "Dad" as I call him, been pressuring me to write one? After all, I have been very sick for the last two years, still working every day, hoping for a diagnosis and treatment. Why would I tackle a monumental project to write an eBook?

Truth Matters

"Life is to be fortified by many friendships. To love and to be loved is the greatest happiness of existence."

*Sydney Smith
(1771-1845)*

Logic tells me, the last thing I need is to add the extra stress of writing a book. The world has thousands of grief, and healing your way through loss, grief books. Yet, on August 23, 2011, I picked up a composition book, a black pen and started to write.

Funny, I started to write my feelings about the loss of a child and a 5.9 earthquake just struck Mineral, Virginia near Washington D.C.

The last time an earthquake of this magnitude hit Virginia was 1897. As I am writing this, officials have evacuated terminal A at Washington Reagan National Airport, the White

House, and adjacent buildings the North Anna Nuclear Power Plant located twenty miles from the epicentre is shut down, all national monuments and parks in Washington have been determined 'stable but closed', with minor injuries and damages being reported.

Amtrak has reported service disruption, cell phone service as far away as New York City was interrupted. The Pentagon began shaking violently and was evacuated. The shaking was felt at the New York Stock Exchange. The National Cathedral in Washington is confirmed to have damage.

One interesting point to note is the earthquake was felt all the way to the New York Stock Exchange, yet traders shouted to each other, "Keep trading!"

When our phone call came in that Saturday evening, June 10, 2006, our world, our family, our faith, our future was shaken to its very core. We were just as shaken as this 5.9 earthquake in Virginia. The similarities are striking. It came without warning and aftershocks were widespread. Damages and injury were sustained. Just as it was on the floor of the New York Stock Exchange, we found the world stops for no one.

We found ourselves frozen in time - as if we were taken hostage and held against our will - in a glass globe, looking out. The world and life in it, continued around us, just like the traders on the Exchange floor no one missed a beat.

People went to work, the grocery, on vacation, played softball games, celebrated July 4th picnics, and prepared to start a new school year in the fall. For a brief moment, everyone in or near the epicentre of the earthquake stopped, and focused on little more than the realization an earthquake had just hit the area.

The earthquake would have a lasting effect on those who sustained property or physical damage. As many as thirty-seven schools in Prince George County closed and some schools were closed until after Labor Day.

Immediately after receiving the phone call from the police officer at the scene of our son's motorcycle accident, our lives and the lives of our immediate family, and Richard's friends, became focused on one thing, Richard.

He didn't pass away at the scene. He sustained traumatic brain injury and traumatic internal injuries. He was stabilized for seventeen hours at the trauma center. The hospital waiting area quickly filled with family and friends holding a vigil for Richard throughout the night, even getting the attention of trauma staff members as the crowd exceeded one hundred supporters. Throughout the night a battle for life was waged.

A severe thunderstorm brewed outside, lightning, thunder, and pouring rain. What I believe was a battle between the planes or the Heavens was taking place. My nephew's wife called my sister, and asked her if it was storming at the hospital and described the powerful storm outside, and told her lightning had just run into the house, striking a toy on the floor causing a bell to ring. Richard's future was in the balance. His right arm and right leg were severely damaged and would face amputation. His dad wrapped a heated towel around his right arm as it turned blue.

Traumatic brain injury offered us a five percent survival rate, and the survival would be a vegetative state, with the remainder of his life spent in a full care nursing facility. His dad stood beside his head, and using the vacuum, removed blood from his mouth as it pooled. The truth is, Richard wasn't coming home.

Richard was twenty-two.

Still living at home, Richard hadn't married yet, and had no children; he was still trying to find his way. Why on this particular Saturday night in June, was Richard's name called? Or did he volunteer? Sure, Richard experienced a few life challenges growing up with Perthese and Juvenile Rheumatoid Arthritis.

The last five years, I have fought the urge to write my feelings. One reason was, I didn't want to expose myself, my pain. I didn't want to reveal the truth, standing naked for all to see. It would be revealing the bleeding, gaping wounds, and the darkness that seeps from the deepest sources of my soul. I am also concerned about our other children. I have to write this to be an encouragement for grieving mothers and I can't do that without being honest.

My children having not lost a child may not be able to understand my feelings. I opted for Truth Matters.

The day I picked up this paper and pen a rare earthquake struck Washington DC.

Now just days into this project, a hundred year storm is preparing to pound the Atlantic East Coast - Hurricane Irene. A category 2 hurricane is taking aim on the entire East Coast. The storm has its sights on New York City. There is 24hour news coverage on the Weather Channel. Washington DC has cancelled the Martin Luther King, JR monument unveiling service which has been years in the making, with crowds in excess of a quarter of a million people expected to attend.

I can't help but wonder as I sit here, how many lives and families will be impacted by the wrath of this storm. Whose life will come to a standstill? Who will find themselves in the glass globe, frozen in time, looking out to the world moving around them? I wonder how many have been separated from the busyness of life, the routines and goals, and the hopes for the future. It will be their new reality.

You've heard the saying, "when life hands you lemons, make lemonade." It's a warm, fuzzy feeling cliché. The truth is lemonade is not a comfort food, I think it's sour. Truth is, when you are in the storm and you are battered and beaten - gaping wounds - the last thing you need is someone dressing that wound with lemonade.

To think you can take the storms of life and transform them into something different is denial in my personal opinion. I don't want to take Richard's life or the accident and dress it up into something else, so I can handle it. You will need to find your own way. It might take you just a short time to find your way and it can take others years and yet for others, they sadly may remain lost. I opted for Truth Matters. True growth from the storm, can only come when we can face our storm and agree to continue on the journey hand in hand, arm in arm with the storm. Like me, you probably read a lot about finding your path, but I now believe, we are the path.

When we become the path the search is over.

It's now just hours after Hurricane Irene, and in the truest form of life, there are some families and communities totally devastated, while others dodged the bullet. Almost two dozen people have been reported killed due to storm related issues. These losses are the highest form of devastation. One of those killed was an eleven year old boy, who was killed by a tree falling on his home. Today, news channels are showing videos of that tree and covered bridges being washed away in Vermont that were constructed in 1870. Poised for almost a hundred and fifty years, and now in 2011, the Universe decides their time is fulfilled.

These family members and communities are left with the daily chores of facing life with significant change.

Permanent change.

I utterly disagree with the cliché, "finding closure". There is a finding of fact, and the journey to learning, so you can function in and with the storm. If there is a love connection between you and that which you lost, it's my belief closure will not come. Love is energy and pure energy never dies.

Just as it is with any deep wound, our bodies will over time begin a scabbing and scarring process. There will be times in our lives, under certain circumstances, this scab will get knocked off and you will bleed. I doubt any two journeys would ever be identical. The variables of the relationship between the people, and the variables to the loss itself, make it impossible to replicate.

Now, days after Hurricane Irene, the storm did not impact communities on the level of disaster anticipated, but it has been the aftermath of the storm that has caused the greatest destruction. The hurricane concern was the slow grind as it made its way up the East Coast. The most serious damage would actually occur hundreds of miles inland and it wouldn't be the hurricane, but flooded rivers throughout New York, Vermont, New Jersey and Maine. One death occurred in New York, when a house swept from its foundation killing a vacationer submerged with the flood waters. In Vermont, a father and son were killed, as they were manning the municipal water system. At one count, at least forty deaths in 11 states are being reported.

I am sharing this detail, to illustrate how the actual event has far reaching implications. This is why I disagree with many of the studies and research on grief. The research is too narrow in its queries. What was a hurricane for some became a flood for others.

The loss is the same, loss. Experiencing the loss of a family member, either through tragedy or illness, is a life altering event. The event may be far reaching for those parents who lose a young adult child in a vehicle accident and the parents' divorce in the aftermath.

The mother, who struggles with grief of losing her child in the war, may get a cancer diagnosis the next year. The one who struggles with guilt over the loss may attempt or succeed with suicide. Days, weeks even years later, as far inland as the flood waters of Hurricane Irene so is the aftermath of loss.

Personally, the first year after Richard's passing; I was withdrawn, elusive, could not sleep, and sought the help of a psychiatrist. Each day felt like a concrete block was attached to each leg, and the weight was unbearable at times. I found myself trying to comfort my husband. Even so, to my dismay, the hands of the clock and the days on the calendar continued to change.

Tick tock, tick tock.

I would visualize physically climbing up, and standing on the hands of the clock, and with all my might trying to stop the hands from advancing. If I could just stop time, just for a minute, just long enough to breath. Stopping time would stop the pain.

Life is all about change, and it never seeks our permission. What life allows us to do is respond, and participate. Life also offers us choices. We can choose the path of resistance, avenue of denial, or the highway of togetherness. Our choices are two to one against the change.

Change is not easy.

It brings uncertainty, fear, anger, and for a few hope. If it were as simple as our response to the change, that would be one thing, but it's not that simple. Our responses come wrapped up in our belief systems, and our cultures. There is no magic prescription or silver bullet for surviving the loss of a child.

Life's journey is testing our endurance, growth, commitment, courage, adaption, flexibility, trust, love, forgiveness, belief, and willingness.

Michael Jackson performed an incredible song titled, "Man in the Mirror." Due to copyright issues I won't quote here, but this is the basic message:

Start with the reflection in the mirror.
Consider a change.

Start with the man in the mirror, a reflection of your true self, the love within you. Ditch the unrealistic, preconceived myths you have about yourself.

Touch, heal, and energize those who cross your path. Be the source of encouragement, and enlightenment providing clarity, focus, and understanding.

Today another mother mourns.

Inconsolable and Indestructible

Since beginning this journey, have you experienced the deluge of unsolicited advice from well-wishers? I truly believe most of the advice is with the best of intentions. How do we process all of this advice? How did you process it? It's not like everyone is saying the same thing, but everyone seems to tweak what they have to offer, with just enough spice to make you wonder if they were on to something. This was one of my biggest battles in the early days after the accident.

I am the one on the mend, and I'm trying to figure out a way to respond without hurting anyone's feelings or seeming brash. You know the face you make, when you try on a new pair of shoes and before your foot ever gets completely in the shoe, you know it's a full size too small? You know before they ever finish their sentence, what they are saying just isn't a fit for you. How did you handle it? Have you lost friendships since the loss of your child? I believe, we all have. This is such a difficult subject and well people like to have answers. It's just our nature to want conclusions and move on. It is easier to move away from something you can't fix, than it is to stay with something broken.

I have a co-worker whose spouse is a veterinarian. They live on a farm and raise sheep. When their children were young and witnessed the birth of a new addition to the family, it was natural to fall in love with the babies. The hard truth is not all of the babies survive. They were faced with children questioning death.

The veterinarian said, "You can't fix dead." I have often wondered how the parent would have responded. I have to admit, I still struggle getting over this reality. You can't fix dead.

I know.

It's true.

It's absolutely true.

My struggle is when it's your dead. Mothers fix things, it's what we do. Remember Zazi, the cheetah, who nurtured her stillborn cub, and continued to groom, and move the stillborn cub, as she cared for the other cubs? Zazi couldn't fix dead either, but it was her response to the stillbirth, that has me in awe of her.

Truth Matters

The difference between the right word,
And the almost right word,
Is the difference between lightning and a lightning bug.

Mark Twain

My struggle was so difficult during the days after auto-pilot shut off. So difficult, that as the grieving mother who needed answers, I started to question areas of life I had never visited before. I shared we had the traditional service and burial. So now I needed to know what next? How long will Richard look like Richard? When does the decomposition process begin? What is the first part of decomposition? Will the fact that Richard was embalmed preserve him, and if so how long?

What I found out was, the more trauma to a body, the less effective the embalming process. If I had this information available to me during those times of decision making, I may have chosen another route, and to be blunt, saved the money. *This was not discussed.*

My mother instinct was revealing itself in a form I never once given a moment's thought to. I wasn't called to be a coroner or a funeral home director. I wasn't called to be a doctor. I knew nothing about the human body, and what happens when the spirit energy has evacuated its shell.

Some people blame the internet for everything. It is a good blame game. My need to know was so intense; I would have visited the local library and searched medical books if I had to. The fear of what I would find as I began this search was at times paralyzing. I remember many times holding my breath and even closing my eyes when I got ready to hit 'enter'.

I needed to know but I didn't want to see. Earlier, I shared the circumstances surrounding the organ donation request. I am an organ donor supporter, and I think what happened to us is a rare situation. If you are still trying to decide how you feel about organ donation, and your struggle is not based on your religious belief, then I would advise you to become a donor. The one thing I have come to terms with is, this body is a tool. A tool in the tool box of Universal progress, and when my job here is finished, I don't need to take this tool box with me.

We don't take office equipment with us when we resign from our jobs. If I can help someone else supply their tool box, in order for them to finish their work, then it's a no brainer for me. It also helped to find out that my organs are going to be depleted, by a very long thin needle to relieve any fluids, if I choose the traditional burial method and I am embalmed. I can't use them like that.

You can't fix dead.

I have decided not to share the very gruesome details of decomposition here. I just thought, it was important to share the thoughts I had in this area, for mothers who may be struggling with these thoughts. I didn't get very far in my search for information. I decided there were some visuals I just didn't need. I didn't need to torture myself; even self-inflicted torture was not going to relieve this pain.

Mark Nepo, a poet, philosopher, and cancer survivor says, *"Everything has changed and nothing has changed."* I can accept that statement when I choose to look at my journey on a Universal level, and not when I am sitting on the couch in my living room. He also noted, after his brush with death, how many books he owned that were useless.

Funny, I have been thinking the same thing. Nepo released a book titled, "*The Book of Awakening*". I haven't read the book yet, yet. Nepo was featured on Oprah's Super Soul Sunday recently, and he said a few things that raised my curiosity. I think he warrants a Google search. One story he shared was, a Hindu teaching I am going to share here. I don't think I am breaking any copyright issues because it appears the original author of the teaching is unknown, and like many teachings passed down by elders through time orally.

A Taste of Wisdom

An aging Hindu master grew tired of his apprentice complaining and so, one morning, sent him for some salt. When the apprentice returned, the master instructed the unhappy young man to put a handful of salt in a glass of water and then to drink it.

"How does it taste?" the master asked.

"Bitter," spit the apprentice.

The master chuckled, and then asked the young man to take the same handful of salt and put it in the lake.

The two walked in silence to the nearby lake and once the apprentice swirled his handful of salt in the water, the old man said, "Now drink from the lake."

As the water dripped down the young man's chin, the master asked, "How does it taste?"

"Fresh," remarked the apprentice.

"Do you taste the salt?" asked the master.

"No," said the young man.

At this the master sat beside the unhappy young man, who so reminded him of himself and said,

"The pain of life is pure salt; no more, no less. The amount of pain in life remains exactly the same. However, the amount of bitterness we taste depends on the container we put the pain in. So, when you are in pain, the only thing you can do is to enlarge your sense of things . . . Stop being a glass. Become a lake."   Author Unknown

Many specialists who have worked with the 5 stages of grief commonly called the 'grief cycle', have since found the stage theory is too simplistic, and have started to look at dynamics, experiences and processes.

John Bowlby, a psychiatrist studying bereavement, is outlining the ebb and flow of the process like, shock and numbness, yearning and searching, disorganization and despair, and reorganization.

I agree, the loss of a child is far too complex an issue, to place in a simplistic box of aged spouses dying from natural causes.

What Now?

What now? Did you find yourself asking this question in the immediate firestorm, and even if it's been a number of years since your loss, are you still asking that same question?

I still ask. What now?

When I began compiling my story, I knew what I wanted the title to be. I wanted it to be what my life has been for the last 5 and one half years. I also picked out a couple of pen names. I really liked Katherine Foster or Katherine Douglas. They seemed so proper and elegant. I even had an eBook cover prepared using Katherine Douglas. I realized through the process of revisiting the events of this journey, I was still hiding. I was still hiding from the reality 5 and one half years later.

I wanted to share what happens behind the composure we exhibit at work and with family, but I wasn't willing to put my name on it because then, I would have to own it. It would be my pain, my struggle and my journey.

It is.

I was still unwilling to accept the personal pain. It is still too raw. I began to follow other grieving parents on a Face Book page and realized I could not run from this pain anymore. Putting a pen name on the book is not going to take the pain away. My hope was in sharing my pain with you it would bring me strength.

It has.

I decided to put my name on the cover and chose to own the pain instead of hiding behind it. How many well-wishers have told you, "Time heals all wounds?" I used to feel that way before suffering taught me a lesson or two. This is another cliché' I refuse to agree with just because it has worked for others. It hasn't worked for me. I don't anticipate it will work for me. How many times during the course of your routine activities does something happen and 'slap' there it is again. The day your life changed forever.

It can be as simple as going to retrieve your mail. A letter arrives addressed to your child. It could be answering the phone, and a telemarketer or bill collector asks to speak to your child. For what feels like hours, you are frozen in milliseconds of time, what now?

Paralyzed with questions of how to respond.

I made dozens of copies of my son's death certificate to attach to and return mail. I've also had a few choice words for callers on the phone. Then, there are the uncomfortable times, when you are in public and everyone is chattering about how great life is, and how the kids are doing, and the achievements everyone is making.

You realize five years later, they have moved on and the memory of your tragedy is but a blip on the screen of their lives. I don't fault them, it's just life and you leave with the heavy feeling of the suffering that refuses to leave your soul. You can't fix dead. The world stops for no one.

Time heals.

No.

Rather, we learn to navigate, maneuver, dodge, climb, crawl, fight, withdraw, duck, and run. This continued movement on our part, is what leads others to believe we are healing. If only it was as easy as spin around three times, click your red, ruby slippers together, and immediately you are transported back to the day before Time rose from its chair and said, "Now."

Truth Matters

"It's said, 'time heals all wounds. I do not agree. The wounds remain, in time, the mind, protecting its sanity, covers them with scar tissue and the pain lessens but it's never gone."

Rose Kennedy
Mother of U.S. President John F. Kennedy, who outlived four of her nine children.

I love that lady.

What now? It has been 2,058 days or 5 years, 7 months and 18 days, of putting one foot in front of the other. Many of those 2,058 days are filled with a dark, empty void, like walking into a room without electricity and no windows. There are days filled with fog, and some memory of my activities. I had my days going without showering and wearing the same clothes three or four days in a row.

Before the accident, I never left the house without my makeup and my hair done. Today, none of that is important. You would find me more times than not, without makeup and wearing sweat pants and sandals. Most days are filled with motion but no "E"-motion. I have found beauty in a few things. We established a Learning & Memorial Butterfly Garden for our community. Other families in the community, who experienced the loss of a child, joined with us as we placed memorial bricks in the garden.

I also participate in a Crock Pot Exchange. I no longer spend money for fresh flowers when a friend passes away. I prepare homemade macaroni and cheese or a nice pot of chili and fill a crock pot. Where I live it is traditional to take food to the family's home. I attach a card to the crock pot, instructing the family NOT to return the crock pot to me after the service, but to fill it with a homemade recipe and deliver to a grieving family in the future. You can easily purchase a new crock pot for under $25, or you can pick up an almost new one at estate sales. This is both economically and environmentally gratifying.

Benjamin Franklin tells us to do something worth writing about or to write something worth reading. I am on the wrong side of thirty, and lack the passion to do anything someone would find interesting enough to write about. Maybe you have found that courage and strength since the loss of your child. I pray you have. If not, I know you have something worth writing about.

You.

An old Latin Proverb says, "Experience is the best teacher."

Truth Matters

"Remembering you on your birthday. Your gift to others was laughter and laughter never dies."

Cynthia Snapp, Richard's Mom

"To be nobody but yourself in a world which is doing its best day and night to make you like everybody else means to fight the hardest battle which any human being can fight and NEVER stop fighting."

E. E. Cummings
(1894-1962)

The Journey

Infancy brings excitement and hope.

First steps and words memorialized.

Dreams of the Tooth Fairy, Santa Claus, and Easter Bunny, birthdays, and Halloween anticipation.

School years, boy scouts, sports, first dance and the high school prom usher out childhood.

First job, W2's, wisdom teeth, road trips, falling in love and friendships.

Willie Nelson, White Snake and Johnny Cash say it best:

Departure brings reflection.

Remembering…

The Children we love so much.

Update

Since releasing this book in 2012, my world and all that I believed to be true has been challenged. Please visit Amazon for information on my newest release:

"Awaken to Our Enchanted Universe"

Made in the USA
Charleston, SC
24 January 2015